LET'S VISIT GERMANY

Let's Visit

Germany

James Moore

BURKE ★ LONDON

First published October 1968
© James Moore 1968

ACKNOWLEDGEMENTS

The author and publishers are grateful to the following individuals and organisations for assistance in preparing this book and for permission to reproduce illustrations: The Press Department of the Federal Republic of Germany; Mrs. Hilda Forman and the Britain–G.D.R. Information Exchange *(Bridge)*; Lex Hornsby & Partners Ltd. (particularly Mr. Forbes Stewart).
The cover photograph of the Rhine Valley is reproduced by permission of Skyport Fotos.

222 69708 3 Library Ed.
222 69707 5 Classroom Ed.

Burke Publishing Company Limited,
14 John Street, London, W.C.1.
Filmset by Keyspools Ltd., Golborne, Lancs.,
and printed by C. Tinling & Co. Ltd., Liverpool, London and Prescot.

Contents

GERMANY

Germany Today

Present-day Germany is a country almost completely surrounded by other nations. Her sea coasts are short, for the most part along the Baltic Sea. Only one very short, but important, stretch looks across the North Sea with the ports of Wilhelmshaven, Bremerhaven and Hamburg. A ship canal, built in 1895 and called the *Nord-Ostsee-Kanal* (better known in English as the Kiel Canal) makes it possible for large ocean-going ships to reach the Baltic without going round the top of Denmark.

No less than nine countries flank Germany's borders. To the west there are Holland, Belgium, Luxembourg and France; to the south Austria and Switzerland; to the east Czechoslovakia and Poland and to the north Denmark.

Germany is by no means a flat country, though a visitor to the north might think so. The North German Plain stretches

A view of the great, flat rolling plain which stretches right across Europe from northern Germany to Russia

the whole way across the country, reaching as far south as Hannover. This great flat area, uninterrupted by more than the smallest of hills and broken up only by changes in country-side, forests and lakes, is part of the vast plain of Northern Europe, which extends the whole way to the Ural Mountains in Russia. Fewer people live there than in other parts of lowland Germany, but there is fine farmland as you go south, towards the mountains.

A large part of the remainder of Germany is mountainous. Firstly, moving south from the North German Plain there are what the Germans call the *Mittelgebirge*. These are the ranges of medium height, rising from 3,000 to 4,000 feet. They include, among others, the Hunsrück, the Eifel, the Taunus and Thuringian Forest, as well as the Harz Mountains, whose highest peak, the Brocken, rises to 3,747 feet, and the Erzgebirge, or Ore Mountains.

Further south still are more mountains mingled with fertile plateaux. Here the most important ranges are the Odenwald, Black Forest, Swabian Alp and the Bavarian Forest. The Feldberg, one of the mountains in the Black Forest, is almost 5,000 feet high.

A typical valley in the pine-clad hills and mountains of the Black Forest

Although many of the regions are called "forests" they are, in fact, thickly forested mountain areas.

All these regions are a delight to the holidaymaker, with wooded uplands, fields, lakes and reservoirs, ancient towns and villages and medieval castles towering on rocky crags. These castles once stood guard against the many warlike princes and are now nearly all hotels, hostels, ancient monuments or museums.

Here, too, there are quiet valleys where, amid the fertile fields, the traveller often sees picturesque half-timbered houses, sometimes whole villages of them. Each region has its own particular design of house by which it can be recognised.

Not all of the valleys are beautiful, however. There is, for example, the valley of the River Ruhr which has more factories than any other region of Germany. There are many large industrial towns, too, but few of them spoil the country in which they stand. Upper Saxony is the second largest industrial area after the Ruhr.

In the very south of the country there are the Alpine foothills and the Bavarian Alps. The scenery here is very like that in Switzerland. The valleys are narrow and deep, and jagged peaks reach up to over 9,000 feet.

Germany's highest mountain, the Zugspitze, is in the Bavarian Alps and is 9,721 feet high. Once again this is a favourite holiday area, especially with walkers and climbers and, in the winter, skiers.

Just to the north of the Bavarian Alps there is the large flat

This picture-book castle is Burg Hohenzollern, the family seat of the Hohenzollern family which provided the kings of Prussia from 1701 to 1918

agricultural region round the basin of the River Danube and its tributaries. Munich, the capital of Bavaria, is near its centre.

There are several large rivers in Germany, all of which are important for transport and communications.

The Danube, Europe's longest river, rises in the Black Forest and flows for 402 miles before it leaves Germany on its way to the Black Sea. However, the most important river in the country is the Rhine which flows for 537 miles through

11

Germany. For hundreds of years this river has been one of Europe's highways, carrying both passengers and goods from the north and south. With its many tributaries, like the rivers Main, Neckar, Moselle, Lahn and Ruhr (most of them navigable for long distances), it serves an immense area of West Germany today. The transport is efficient and cheap for raw materials such as oil and coal, and manufactured goods. Most of the passengers these days are holidaymakers.

Another great German river is the River Oder which forms the eastern boundary with Poland and flows for nearly five hundred miles before it reaches the Baltic Sea at the Polish

The craggy, snow-clad Bavarian Alps—a favourite holiday area. The range includes the Zugspitze, Germany's highest mountain

A beautiful horseshoe-shaped stretch of the River Saar, one of the tributaries of the Moselle

port of Szcecin. Finally there is the River Elbe, which flows from Upper Saxony to Hamburg and is very important as a commercial waterway.

The larger part of Germany has changeable weather just like most Western Europe. However, further east the climate is more extreme: the winters tend to be colder and the summers hotter. Rain falls at all times of the year (but not all the time, of course) and, with one-quarter of the country covered with dense forest, Germany is a green and pleasant land.

A Glimpse of the Past

Germania was the name given to the land across the Rhine by the Romans who invaded the country under Julius Caesar in the first century B.C. There are still signs of the Roman occupation to be seen today in such towns as Aachen and Trier, where the Roman legions were stationed.

Although this is a fascinating chapter in Germany's history we shall start our story proper in the Middle Ages, about eight hundred years after the birth of Christ. For it was in A.D. 800 that the Emperor Charlemagne, Charles the Great, received his crown from Pope Leo III and settled down at Aachen to rule the Holy Roman Empire, whose citizens were the German-speaking Lower Saxons, Frisians, Franks, Thuringians, Swabians and Bavarians.

Under Charlemagne and his successors, known as the

14

Evidence of the Romans is still to be found in parts of Germany. This impressive gateway, at Trier, once formed part of the Roman walls of the city

Carolingians, Germany became a largely Christian country. During the next five hundred years the small states which made up the empire gradually grew bigger. In a comparatively peaceful atmosphere the towns grew in size and prosperity and the country as a whole became more powerful.

At the same time, however, the princes who ruled the states also became more powerful and began to quarrel over who should rule the empire. In the years immediately following A.D. 1250 the Pope persuaded the seven princes responsible for choosing the ruler (they were called the "Electors") to find a new emperor. This they did in 1273. They chose Rudolph of Hapsburg, whose descendants were to remain most promi-

15

nent among Germany's rulers for over four hundred years, until 1806, in fact; and then in Austria until 1914.

In all this time, though, Germany was far from peaceful. Many of the wars were religious ones. Perhaps the most serious of all was the so-called Thirty Years War (1616–1648). This was a bloodthirsty conflict between the Catholics and the Protestants, during which large parts of central Germany became a battlefield. There are many walled cities and fortresses remaining in Germany today as a reminder of those grim times.

Then came the struggles with Austria and France in the eighteenth century when King Frederick the Great of Prussia (who reigned from 1740–1786), perhaps the most widely known of all German rulers, made his state into the most effective military power in Germany. At the same time he passed new laws to ensure that his people were better fed and that the country became rich. He built a fine new city— Berlin—and marched his troops to victory after victory.

The Holy Roman Empire finally came to an end in 1806 when it was attacked and effectively defeated by the French armies under Napoleon. In 1813 thirty-two states were again joined together to make the country now known as Germany. In 1871 these states formed the German Reich (Empire) under the rule of the King of Prussia, William II. In that year Germany utterly defeated France (in the Franco–Prussian War) and thereby established herself as the strongest military power in Europe.

Cologne Cathedral. Its foundations had already been laid at the time when Rudolph of Hapsburg became emperor in 1273—but the building was not finished for another six hundred years!

The palace of Sans Souci at Potsdam, built by Frederick the Great. This elaborate and graceful building expressed the power and prosperity of the Prussians under their most famous king

The first chancellor of the German Reich was Otto von Bismarck (1815–1898) and under his control the country grew prosperous. She became respected throughout the world for her successes in all fields—science, industry, economics and culture—gradually rising to be recognised as one of the leading powers of Europe.

Unfortunately, Germany's growing power resulted in her joining forces with Austria to wage war on Russia in 1914 (the First World War), a war in which France and Great Britain were soon involved. The U.S.A. also joined in against Germany in 1917. Although Russia was defeated by Germany and Austria, in the end the Germans lost the war to the Allies. The peace treaty which was signed at Versailles in 1919 was very harsh. It called upon Germany to pay large amounts of money to the countries she had fought. Many of her industries were crippled by having their machinery taken away. In addition, the railway system was seriously hampered by the removal of engines and rolling-stock. The German people faced mass unemployment and poverty.

In these very bad conditions a new political party arose called the National Socialist Party (Nazi for short—from the German name *N*ationalso*z*ialist), led by an Austrian named Adolf Hitler. By great political skill and using a certain amount of force, exerted by a large private army called the Brownshirts, Hitler managed to have himself elected chancellor of Germany in 1933. His National Socialist Party now became the only political force in the country and Hitler became dictator. This evil and ruthless man was soon planning to extend German rule over all German-speaking parts of Europe, and beyond. With great speed the armed forces were built up to peak strength, while other countries in Europe stood by and tried to negotiate rather than face Germany on the battlefield.

In 1939 Germany attacked Poland. Poland's allies, Great Britain and France, had no choice but to declare war on

Germany and so the Second World War broke out. It was a terrible war. The Nazis, spurred on by Hitler who frequently acted as though mad, were responsible for some truly hideous crimes. Perhaps the worst of these was the putting to death of several million innocent people, most of them Jews. More than one attempt was made to assassinate Hitler and replace his devilish government, but it was not until the Allied Armies had occupied most of Germany by force that he finally committed suicide and the country was allowed to return to normality. In 1945 Germany was again utterly defeated. Widespread destruction of German property had taken place as a result of the war. Whole cities—Berlin, Leipzig, Dresden, Hamburg and Stuttgart—as well as the industrial centres of

One of the worst-hit cities in the Second World War was Dresden, seen in this photograph in October 1946

the Ruhr and Saxony lay in ruins, with their roads and railways almost useless. Germany's working men had been called up into the armed forces and millions of them had been killed or taken prisoner, especially on the Russian front. Consequently, Germany was without a proper labour force to work her industries and farm her land.

The problems of the first few years after the war were great indeed. Germany was forced to start almost from scratch.

To ensure that the defeated country was properly administered, it was divided into four zones of military government and was occupied jointly by Great Britain, France, the U.S.A. and Russia. Three of these zones now comprise the German Federal Republic, colloquially known as West Germany, a democratic, capitalist state under a republican government—with the president as head of state.

The Russian-controlled zone has now become the German Democratic Republic, or G.D.R., known as East Germany, a socialist state with a communist government.

Thus the old Germany of 1937 is now split into two countries with very different forms of government. The present areas do not quite make up that of the Germany of pre-war days since the lands east of the rivers Oder and Neisse are occupied by Poland who claimed them by ancient right.

The recovery of West Germany is often described as the *economic miracle*, for her people are now not only better off than before the war, but have one of the highest standards of living in Europe. This is due very largely to their hard work, but also to the great amount of help given to the country by the U.S.A., France and Great Britain.

East Germany's struggle has been somewhat harder for several reasons. Natural resources are very small in East Germany and the working population has actually grown smaller since the war. East Germany is the only country in Europe whose population has gone down in recent years. Moreover, the number of old people is very high by comparison with the workers.

Despite these difficulties East Germany is now the fifth largest industrial country in Europe and the ninth in the world. It can rightly be claimed that the G.D.R.'s recovery has been an economic miracle too, even if the people are still not as well off as those in West Germany.

Finally, a few words must be said about Berlin. Although the whole city is situated well within the borders of the G.D.R., more than half of it belongs to the West, to the German Federal Republic. But the eastern part of the city is the capital of the G.D.R. Since officially no diplomatic relations exist between East and West Germany, maintaining West Berlin as part of the West has always been a difficult matter. It can only be reached along certain permitted routes through East Germany and its $2\frac{1}{4}$ million people have often, in recent years, been the centre of disputes. For West Germany the city is a showpiece in the centre of a country of whose policies she is critical. For the G.D.R. it is like having strangers occupying part of their house without permission. We do not know what

Now the signs of war have completely disappeared and new buildings have sprung up everywhere. These are new flats in a residential area of East Berlin

the future will bring for Berlin, but we can be sure that we have not heard the last of the problems which the divided city poses.

People at Work

Nearly fifty-nine million people live in the Federal Republic of Germany, whose capital is Bonn on the River Rhine. Of these, $2\frac{1}{4}$ million live in West Berlin. Apart from Berlin, the largest city in the Federal Republic is Hamburg, followed by Munich, both with over one million people.

The German Democratic Republic is only two-fifths the size of the Federal Republic. It has seventeen million inhabitants. The capital is Berlin and the next largest cities are Dresden and Leipzig with just over half a million people each.

The Germans are known throughout the world as hard-working people. It is a kind of national characteristic. No matter where Germans go in the world they take this reputation with them. Of course, there are lazy Germans just as there are lazy people in every other country, but on the whole they are a very industrious race. You may think that this would make them dull people, but far from it. They enjoy themselves a great deal. But work comes first.

This is the reason why the West Germans enjoy the highest standard of living in Europe today and the East Germans, in spite of having a country which is poor in natural resources, are quite prosperous, too. It is only because of this ability to work hard and to work together as a team that the German people have twice in the last sixty years been able to build their country up again after being defeated in war. In 1945, at the end of the Second World War, the country was like a vast heap of ruins and many people were left penniless. Ten years later most of the ruined cities and factories had been rebuilt. Today everybody is better off than ever. People in other countries who were watching what was going on called it a miracle.

The traditional skills of the German people are famous. From earliest times, German craftsmen carved in wood, built cathedrals and palaces, and made beautiful pottery; their work was greatly admired. As times changed and modern industries came into being, new skills were developed and were put to other uses, such as the making of motor cars and cameras. In this way, Germany became recognised as a country with great engineering skill. Germans are, for the most part, careful workmen who enjoy doing a job properly,

The West-Berliners worked hard to rebuild their city. Now they enjoy its elegance and prosperity

and German workmanship has always been held in high esteem the world over.

With these advantages it is small wonder that Germany is today one of the great industrial countries of the world. Both East and West Germany export large quantities of everything they make to all parts of the world. Of course, their customers are not the same countries. East Germany sends most goods to Russia (her biggest single customer) and certain other Communist countries, such as Czechoslovakia, Poland and Bulgaria, with whom she has special friendly relations. A great deal of her output also goes to West Germany. In fact, most countries in the world import some East German goods.

West Germany sells most of her exports to other Western European countries, especially those which are also members

The Germans are renowned for their hand-decorated china. Here a young artist is painting a traditional pattern on a piece of Meissen-ware

A woodcarver in Oberammergau, Bavaria, where no less than five hundred craftsmen work, producing figures such as this for exporting to all parts of the world

of the Common Market (France, Italy, Belgium, Luxembourg and Holland). France is the largest single customer. Many exports go to the U.S.A. too, but again there are few countries in the world which do not import some West German goods.

In return, Germany buys many of the raw materials she needs for industry, materials such as iron ore, petroleum, wool and cotton. She also imports supplies of foodstuffs for her people, since the country does not have enough agricultural

27

produce to satisfy all her needs. About one-third of all West Germany's food has to be imported; for East Germany the proportion is much less. It is only in such things as tropical and sub-tropical fruits (oranges, lemons, bananas and the like) that East Germany is completely dependent on imports. These are, however, regarded as luxuries there and are very expensive.

The most important factor then in German industry is skilled labour. There *are* local raw materials, but they are not found in very great quantities. The most important of them is coal. This is mined in two forms: hard or black coal; and lignite, which is soft or brown coal. Nearly all the hard coal, which is the more valuable, is found in West Germany,

As in many industrial countries, the manufacturing centres are to be found where there is coal. The main industrial area in West Germany is the Ruhr where this aerial picture of a coalmine was taken

mainly in the Ruhr. It is estimated that there is enough of it there to satisfy industry's needs for another four hundred years. The vast deposits of lignite in East Germany are expected to last about as long. Lignite, or brown coal, has to be specially treated to make it usable by industry, and in East Germany there are plants for doing this. This processing of lignite was one of the major problems which the East Germans had to solve in building up their industry.

Iron ore, which is another essential raw material for modern industry, is found in both East and West Germany, though the quality of these deposits is not the best. Nor is the quantity ideal. There is only sufficient iron ore in Germany for about one-third of the iron and steel requirements. The rest must be imported, either as ore or as pig iron (large blocks of iron already smelted), or some form of steel.

One of the most important raw materials for Germany's industry is potash, which is widely used in the manufacture of chemicals. The German potash output is roughly one-quarter of the world's total. Germany's chemical industry is, not surprisingly therefore, one of the world's largest.

Copper, lead and zinc are also mined, but there are few other minerals. The only other natural resource which is constantly being increased by man's own efforts is water-power. In both West and East Germany the waters of many rivers are dammed and used to produce electricity.

Germany has few people without jobs. In both the East and

the West a high percentage of women, both married and single, go to work. This is certainly connected with the fact that in wartime, when most of the men were away fighting, the women worked in a variety of jobs. When the war was over, women still had to work because there was a shortage of manpower again; many men had been killed or badly injured in the war. At present, women make up one-third of the working population in West Germany. Recently there have been even more women going to work, mostly married ones trying to earn some extra money. In East Germany the number is even higher. There, women do almost every kind of job

This woman farmworker is doing a job that might be considered man's work in other countries

including manual work like operating machines or driving tractors.

Many families in East Germany depend on the wages of both parents. This results in problems when it comes to caring for the children during the working day.

Since the Second World War Germany has had a shortage of workers. In East Germany the population as a whole actually decreased for several years after the war. This is exactly the opposite of what is wanted in a country which is growing or recovering from a disaster. Many skilled people left the country to go to West Germany where conditions, at least at the time, were much better. West Germany, on the other hand, has solved her labour problem by employing so-called "guest workers", in particular those from other Common Market countries. In recent years there have been as many as $1\frac{1}{4}$ million of them, about twenty-five per cent of them from Italy. They have mostly done manual jobs such as building houses, flats, factories and roads. Not very many of them stay in Germany; most of them go back home when they have earned enough to save some money. East Germany has had to solve her labour problem by asking her people to work harder or by introducing more machinery, which is a very expensive solution.

What goods does German industry produce? If you were to look around the shops to see which things come from Germany you would probably come to the conclusion that most German workers must be employed in making cars (Volkswagen, Mercedes, Wartburg), motor-cycles (N.S.U.), toys—especially mechanical ones—cameras, radios and tape-recorders, textiles, glass, china, tools and electrical goods such as refrigerators and food-mixers.

Cars are probably the product for which Germany is best known to ordinary people throughout the world. One make, the Volkswagen (the name means: "People's Car") is one of the most famous cars ever made. It is affectionately called the "Beetle" because it looks like one. In fifteen years it has hardly changed in appearance, and more "Beetles" have been made than any other car in the world. The Volkswagen company was, until a short time ago, the largest single motor-car company in Europe. Its main factory is at Wolfsburg, near the East-German frontier.

But, even so, things like cars and cameras make up only a very small part of what the Germans manufacture. Much more important are the heavy engineering works which make such things as large presses for shaping steel plates; printing presses; textile machines; giant excavators; bridges; diesel engines for ships; turbines and sugar cane mills, to name but a few. Most of this machinery is used in other countries to make the goods which are sold in the shops.

Many people work, too, in the German chemical industry making medicines, fertilisers, plastics and man-made fibres. A lot of these items are exported, but a great deal finds its way into the home factories to be used as raw materials and

The Volkswagen is Germany's most famous car. Here, whole trainloads of "Beetles" are seen leaving the main factory at Wolfsburg

made into things which the German people themselves want to buy in their shops.

In both East and West Germany shipbuilding is important. All kinds of ships—giant tankers, fishing-boats, cargo ships, passenger- and car-ferries—are built at ports like Bremerhaven, Hamburg, Kiel, Wismar, Rostock and Stralsund.

The greatest number of factories all grouped in one area in West Germany is to be found in the province of North Rhine Westphalia, especially along the River Ruhr, a tributary of the Rhine. The Germans themselves call it the "coal-pot", because coal-mining is the most important feature of the region and all the other industries were built up around it.

33

This is mostly heavy industry: steel-works and chemical plants and giant factories like the Krupp works at Essen, making everything from steel bridges to ships' diesel engines. There are also cotton mills, factories making electrical goods, rubber, cars, locomotives, and machine tools, as well as glass works and leather-manufacturing plants.

Many important manufacturing towns lie on the banks of

Germany is one of the world's leading shipbuilding nations. In this picture a pre-fabricated bow is being fitted to a new 190,000-ton super-tanker in Kiel

other rivers, especially along the rivers Rhine and Main, and particularly on the stretch from Mainz to Karlsruhe. The centre of the German chemical industry is here, at the twin towns of Mannheim–Ludwigshafen.

Southern Germany is thought by most people to be less industrialised than the northern regions. It is often regarded solely as holiday country, but there are factories here, too. No heavy industry, though; no belching chimneys, slag heaps or nasty smells. In southern Germany the people are mainly employed in light industry. There are timber mills, printing works, and factories making cars, electrical goods, dresses, watches and furniture. The main manufacturing towns are Stuttgart, Ulm, Augsburg and Munich. But hardly any town, no matter how small, is without a factory of some kind.

East Germany has most of its factories in the south, in the region called Upper Saxony, which has been an important industrial area for 150 years, second only to the Ruhr. Chemicals are very important here, and the largest factory in East Germany is in the area: the Walter Ulbricht chemical works at Leuna, where over 30,000 people work. A great variety of industries, light and heavy engineering mostly, are found in nearly all the towns. The main centres are Magdeburg, Halle, Leipzig, Erfurt, Zwickau, Karl-Marx-Stadt (once called Chemnitz) and Dresden. Dresden and Meissen are known, too, throughout the world for their china-ware, while Leipzig is internationally famous for its trade fairs which first started eight hundred years ago.

The Walter Ulbricht chemicals factory at Leuna, the largest industrial plant in East Germany

It would be difficult indeed to make a list of all the numerous things which are made in East Germany today. In fact, over six hundred new industries have been started in East Germany since 1946, and today it must be regarded as one of the world's most progressive industrial countries.

Of course, not all the German people work in factories, mines or offices, or on building-sites. There are still many farmers and farm-workers in Germany, though the numbers are getting smaller as agriculture becomes more up-to-date and mechanical equipment is more widely used.

In West Germany there are still many small farms. The average farm has only twenty acres, but many are much smaller. It may seem strange in such a modern state that farming should be run in an inefficient and outdated way. The fact is that to own a piece of land is thought by many people to be more important than having a good wage.

In addition, a great number of people have gardens or

There are still many small farms in West Germany. These peasant farmers are taking their cows across Lake König in the Bavarian Alps to the mountain pastures for the summer

allotments, often outside the towns in which they live, on which they grow flowers and vegetables. Many families build summer-houses in their gardens and at week-ends they go out to spend the day working there.

All kinds of crops are grown but the most important farming products are milk, butter, cheese and meat. Chickens are the most numerous animals, with pigs second and cattle third. Grain, especially rye and wheat, is the main crop, but many vegetables, particularly potatoes, are grown too.

Fruit trees and bushes flourish everywhere in Germany, but more especially in the south. Home-grown fruit is seen much more often in the local shops and markets than it is in other European countries. Of special interest are the vineyards where grapes are grown for wine-making. Although Germany is not at the top of the list of the grape-growing countries for the quantity of the wine she produces, she certainly stands very high for quality, especially of white wine. The white wines of the sunny slopes of the Moselle and Rhine valleys are world famous. Vines are grown in a great many other places in southern Germany, too; particularly in the river valleys of the Main and Neckar, but these wines are not as well known outside Germany as Rhine or Moselle wines.

Though it is still possible to see peasants ploughing with oxen in West Germany this kind of farming is fast disappearing as the government encourages the use of farm machinery. Government plans also include schemes for several farmers to combine and form larger farm units.

Vine-growing on the slopes above the Moselle valley

The most important farming area of East Germany is in the central region, around Magdeburg. East Germany used to have a similar farming system to that of West Germany, with many small peasant farmers. However, it soon became obvious that such a system could not produce enough food for the country. Since the East German government could not afford to import food it persuaded all the farmers to join together in co-operative farms. In this way farming can be

Harvesting sugar beet, a job which used to be done by hand. Note the young boy helping

done on a large scale and by modern methods, including the use of tractors and other farm machinery. Only a very small part of the land is still farmed by individual families on their own, and they are mostly market-gardeners or fruit-farmers.

Animal farming is just as important in the East as in West Germany, though the quantities of livestock are smaller. The main farm crops are wheat, barley, potatoes, maize and sugar beet. Some vines are also grown in East Germany, mainly near Leipzig and Dresden, but the wine-growing is on a very small scale in the East.

The country plans to grow all its own food by 1970.

Road, Rail and River

Germany has one of the finest networks of roads, railways and waterways in the world. Taking into account the length of the railway lines and the size of the country, Germany is only surpassed in this respect by Belgium. The system of motorways, called *Autobahnen*, is the best and longest in Europe and has been copied by all the neighbouring countries. As for the rivers and canals, they enable heavy goods to be taken through the length and breadth of the country, as well as providing wonderful scenic routes for tourists who want to see Germany at their leisure.

The motorways, started in the 1930s mainly for military purposes, join all the most important towns and regions of West Germany as well as some in East Germany. To travel from Munich to Hamburg by motorway (550 miles) only

41

takes about ten hours in a normally fast car. It would be difficult to imagine how the large numbers of cars in Germany would move about today without these roads. They all have dual carriageways, each with two lanes, though the latest ones have three lanes. Some of the more recent *Autobahn* stretches even have four lanes where they go uphill so that the slowest traffic can move right over and allow the faster vehicles to

For centuries rivers have provided the main lines of communication in Germany. This picture clearly demonstrates how modern roads and railways follow the river valleys

An example of the way in which the *Autobahnen* cut straight through the countryside, overcoming all obstacles

pass at their own speed. This is very necessary because one of the most common sights on German motorways is a long queue of lorries, many with trailers, crawling along, laden with goods for shops and factories.

As in other countries, stopping on the motorways is only allowed at special parking places, or at filling-stations and restaurants, which are to be found at regular intervals. Very slow vehicles, such as mopeds, are not allowed to travel on the *Autobahn* at all, because they would hold up the traffic, nor are pedestrians allowed to walk alongside it or cross it. One thing drivers have to avoid is overshooting the place

Flyovers and complicated junctions, such as these in West Berlin, have been devised to prevent traffic jams

where they want to turn off the *Autobahn*, because turning in the road is forbidden and anyone who overshoots has to go on to the next junction, which may be many miles ahead.

The *Autobahnen* are so popular for long-distance travel that even they become overcrowded. On the busiest stretches—between Cologne and Frankfurt, or Frankfurt and Karlsruhe, for example—week-end drivers are often stuck in traffic jams for hours.

The German railways are still most important for dealing with heavy goods traffic. Many through trains going to other countries have to cross Germany, since she is situated more or less in the centre of Europe. This is one of the main reasons why Germany has such a good railway network. Trains from Holland, Belgium and France, going to such places as Poland and Russia, Austria and even as far as Istanbul, have to travel right across Germany. Some of them have romantic names like *Mozart Express*, *Hellas Express* and *Orient Express*. These long-distance passenger expresses are very modern and comfortable and have sleeping- and restaurant-cars. Going by train through Germany is a very interesting and enjoyable way of travelling, since the trains pass through such beautiful countryside. One of the finest trips is down the valley of the River Rhine in the *Rhinegold Express*, which has an all-glass observation car.

So far, only about one-fifth of the railway system is electrified. A large part of the rolling-stock is pulled by diesel

A modern high-speed diesel-hydraulic express. This train can reach a speed of a hundred miles an hour

engines, but there are still many steam trains about. If the present plans are carried through, however, they will all be gone by 1975.

One or two German cities have underground railways. The largest and best-known is that in Berlin which is very like the London Underground or Paris *Métro*. There is another in Hamburg, and new ones are being built or planned in other German cities. Recently a short underground railway was completed in Cologne, and a large one is under construction in Frankfurt where the town's tramways are being led underground.

Trams, by the way, are still quite a common sight on German streets, though as traffic gets heavier it becomes more and more necessary to replace them with buses. Most German trams look very modern; they are low and stream-lined. There is more space in them for standing passengers than for people sitting down. In this way they can carry more passengers in all than they could if they were full of seats. To cope with all the traffic in busy cities two or even three carriages have to be linked together. In the old days, when trams still had doors that could be left open, it was quite a common sight to see them so crowded in the rush hours that clusters of people hung on for dear life, standing on the running-boards outside the doors. Today doors are automatically operated and they close with a hiss on anyone who might be tempted to squeeze in at the last moment. Quite often, when there are two or three carriages, the last carriage has no conductor and is used only by passengers with season tickets. Conductors on German trams (and buses, for that matter) sit at a small desk at the back, by the door through which passengers get on. People pay their fares and then pass along the carriage. They get off through another door at the front.

With the exception of Berlin buses, which look strangely like the double-decker buses in London, German buses are more like long-distance coaches. They are single-deckers and are usually rather long so that they can carry as many passengers as possible. A whole fleet of long-distance buses, painted dark red, is run by the Federal German railways to places which are not served by rail. The most romantic bus service is the one operated by the West German postal authorities in the mountains of south Germany. These buses, which are bright yellow, run a regular service over the alpine roads, delivering mail and carrying huge numbers of holiday-makers, especially in winter.

All Germany's major rivers can be navigated by ships which carry cargo as well as passengers. The most important river by far is the Rhine, which connects Basel (in Switzerland) with the North Sea and is used by ships which carry 2,000 tons or more. Sometimes the water in the upper reaches of the river is very shallow, but a large canal now runs beside the Rhine from Strasbourg (in France) to Basel, enabling the river transport to be used all the year round. At all times of the year the German radio broadcasts reports of the amount of water in all the navigable rivers. These keep the barge-skippers informed of the actual situation at any given moment.

The traffic on the River Rhine is so heavy that sometimes it looks more like a busy road, with ships going up and down in a continuous stream. One of the most interesting places to watch this procession is in the Rhine Gorge just below Bingen, where the river is very narrow and the current extremely strong. Many of the barges have their own engines, but a lot are still pulled or pushed by tugs. It is most exciting to see them struggle against the stream, sometimes only just going fast enough—with their large loads of coal, stone or oil—to make headway.

Some of the Rhine towns, such as Duisburg, Mannheim-

Ludwigshafen and Basel, have ports which are as busy as those on the sea coasts. The tributaries of the Rhine are nearly as busy. The rivers Moselle, Main and Neckar all have locks and are used by many barges, too. Stuttgart, at the head of navigation of the River Neckar, far inland and hundreds of miles from the sea, is a major port.

The River Elbe, which flows through East Germany from Czechoslovakia, is important for the transport of goods to and from the industrial centres of Upper Saxony. It is connected to the River Weser in West Germany by a canal called

A barge being pulled by tug in a lock on a canalised stretch of the Moselle

There are fleets of white-painted passenger-steamers such as these on most German lakes and rivers

the Mittelland Canal, and to Berlin by another man-made waterway.

Canals are not as extensive as rivers in the German waterway system, but one of the most important canals of all time is now under construction in Germany. It will run, when finished, from the River Main across the hills to the River Danube. Cargo ships will then be able to travel right across Europe from the North Sea to the Black Sea. There was once a canal along this route, called the Ludwig Canal in honour of the king who had it built, but it was shallow and it fell into such a bad state of repair that it had to be closed. Another well-known German canal is the Kiel Canal which joins the North Sea to the Baltic Sea. It is one of the busiest ship canals in the whole world.

Goods are not the only things which travel by water in Germany. One of the best ways to see the country is on the rivers in one of the many comfortable passenger ships. Complete with restaurants, bars and sleeping-cabins, several large ships make regular four- or five-day trips up and down the Rhine, calling at many towns on the way. This is a wonderful way to get to know the river and its varied life as well as to

A dramatic aerial view of Hamburg, the most important seaport in Germany. In the foreground is the huge new cargo installation, one of the largest in the world

visit the ancient towns on its banks. Similar ships ply on the River Elbe, taking passengers right into Czechoslovakia on seven-day voyages. Excursion steamers are found on all the other rivers, too, and on many of the lakes of southern Germany.

West Germany also has a very large merchant navy with nearly 4,000 ocean-going ships. These carry goods from other countries besides Germany and are used by all countries in the world. East Germany, which had only one ship after the war, now has a small fleet of cargo- and passenger-ships. They are very modern and efficient, and are used mainly for trading in East Germany's imports and exports. It is interesting to note that in actual numbers far more vessels ply on the inland waterways than go to sea, though the inland ships are naturally much smaller.

Finally, there are the airways. There are several important airfields in Germany, including the international airports at Frankfurt, Hamburg, Berlin and Munich. Germany is a stopping-place for most of the world's major airlines, and she is connected with almost every country in the world by regular flights. The West German airline is called *Lufthansa*; the East German one is known as *Interflug*. There are also a great number of internal flights between German towns, the largest number being between West German airports and Berlin. Owing to the difficulties in travelling by land across East German territory many West Germans prefer to fly to Berlin, and quite a lot of goods are carried that way, too.

52

Schools and Education

Both East and West Germany attach great importance to preparing children for their future adult life by giving them proper schooling. Great care is taken to ensure that there are full opportunities for all children whatever their talents or their handicaps. There are, therefore, special schools of all kinds, and learning does not finish when a boy or girl leaves school to go to work. They often continue going to school part-time in one of the many day- or evening-institutes which are specially run for this purpose.

Naturally, in a country where learning is thought to be so essential, teachers have a high standing. They are paid well and are regarded by most people—parents and children alike —as some of the most important people in the country. To be a teacher in Germany is to have a position of great responsibility and trust, and so teachers have to go through a very long and careful training.

There is close co-operation between teachers and parents in German schools. In East Germany every school has its parents'

53

New schools like this one are being built each year to accommodate the growing population

committee. This does not run the school but it enables teachers and parents to meet and discuss the children's problems frequently.

Discipline in the schools is generally very strict, and children study hard for their exams. In Germany it is vital for everyone who wishes to work to have a definite training. It is interesting to note that shop assistants, for example, have to learn their trade at school and must hold a certificate to show that they know their job.

In both parts of Germany the law states that children have to go to school from the age of six. In East Germany the minimum time for them to stay at school is ten years; in West Germany it is either eight or nine years, depending on the local laws in different parts of the country. After leaving school, West German teenagers have to attend special part-time educational courses until they are eighteen. In East Germany children aged thirteen and upwards have to spend one day a week in a factory or workshop or on a farm so that they get to know at first hand how things are produced

An open-air class in progress in one of West Germany's newly-built schools

and what materials are used. This is a very useful kind of practical schooling.

Lessons in German schools normally start at 8 a.m. and end at 1.30 p.m. Meals are not served in schools; instead the pupils bring sandwiches and fruit which they eat during a 15- or 20-minute mid-morning break. In some towns and villages in West Germany there is so much overcrowding in schools that they work in shifts, and so some pupils go to school from 1.30 to 6 p.m.

Finishing early is very useful for the teachers who can mark books and prepare work in the afternoons. The pupils can have their homework done by teatime and spend their evenings on sports and hobbies. Of course, it may not be quite so good for mothers whose peace and quiet at home ends at 2 p.m.

The East German school system is what is known as comprehensive. After the kindergarten, which is not compulsory but has become part of the school system, all children go to the high school where they are then taught according to their ability and special talents. There are also vocational and trade schools for further education in the most important industries. Engineering and technical schools include art and music in their courses, and there are special factory- and farm-colleges for adults. Evening classes in East Germany are very popular. In recent years even quite elderly important people, such as cabinet ministers, have gone back to school. That shows how important education is in East Germany.

All children in East Germany learn Russian from the fifth

Schoolchildren are encouraged to spend their spare time creatively. These children are holding an exhibition in a square in East Berlin. The passers-by are giving their criticisms

form (when they are ten years old), and two years later they start to learn another foreign language, usually English. The use of visual aids, including television, is very widespread. One of the main features of the East German education system is the belief in the importance of children liking and being able to do practical work as well as put their noses into books. This is why woodwork, metalwork, and engineering are taught to all pupils. It is interesting that, as a result, many girls are persuaded to take up technical occupations.

Recently, special schools have been started in East Germany to take the most gifted children so that they can learn faster. Great attention is also being paid to specialised training for young people to enable them to grasp the most recent technical developments.

In East Germany a great deal of damage was done to school buildings during the Second World War when many were completely destroyed. As a result there are now many new schools—fine buildings built specially to fit in with modern methods of teaching and to include all the latest equipment. This is true, too, of West Germany, but less money has been spent there on new schools.

As in East Germany, schooling in West Germany is free and run by the State, although there are some private schools for those who wish to pay for their children's education. These private schools have special licences and are supervised by the State. In country districts many schools are "one-teacher schools", where pupils of all ages—from six to fourteen—are taught together in one large room by one teacher.

The main difference in the education systems in the two parts of Germany lies in the general arrangement of schools. The comprehensive system does not exist in the West. Instead children have four years at an elementary school, followed by six years at an intermediate school or a secondary school. The secondary school is called a *Gymnasium*, and there are three different kinds. One specialises in modern languages (English, Russian, French, etc.), another in classical languages (Greek and Latin), and a third in mathematics and natural sciences for those who want to become scientists. In this way children of all abilities and interests can go to the schools which teach the subjects they need.

There are many more men teachers than women teachers

The most up-to-date methods of education are being used throughout Germany. This picture shows an electronic teaching system in operation. The lesson is recorded on tape, and the pupils can play it over as often as necessary

in West Germany. In fact, there are about twice as many men as there are women. This means that even girls' schools are often staffed by men, though the head-teacher is normally a woman. Most schools for boys, though, have nearly all men teachers.

It is easy to see that learning is one of the most important parts of life in modern Germany. The school system in Germany has been studied by many countries in the world, in particular by Great Britain and America, and is regarded by many as a model to be copied.

People at Play

The Germans have a reputation for being very hard-working; but, of course, they do not work all the time. Like most civilised people they have free time in the evenings and at week-ends, and then they really like to enjoy themselves.

What do people in Germany do with their leisure time? Well, it naturally depends on their age-group, but there is one pastime which is popular with everybody, no matter what age: and that is walking and hiking. Those who cannot go far afield stroll through the local parks (all the large towns have beautiful parks) or the streets of their town or village, just for the fun of it and to enjoy the fresh air. Others go by train or car out into the countryside; wearing sturdy walking shoes, and carrying rucksacks or picnic bags, they set off to roam the forests, meadows and river valleys in order to enjoy the view, pick wild flowers, or visit an old ruin or popular beauty spot.

Hiking has a long tradition in Germany, and there are many alpine clubs and hiking clubs which organize walking tours

60

for their members in every part of the country. Some of the tours are long and strenuous, especially if they lead into the mountains—the Bavarian Alps or the Black Forest, for example —where these clubs have simple but comfortable huts in which hikers can stay overnight. Young people out on hikes can, of course, also stay in Youth Hostels. There are a great number of these all over Germany; some very modern, others installed in old castles. It is not essential, however, to belong to a club to go hiking, for everybody can find their way about by buying one of the many maps published for hikers and following the coloured signs marked along footpaths.

Young people who find that hiking is too "tame" for them go rock-climbing in the mountains of central or southern Germany. In fact, Germans are among the best rock-climbers in the world and have been the first to conquer some of the most difficult mountains. It was a German climbing team which made the first ascent of the North Face of the Eiger (a formidable mountain in Switzerland). They have also sent many expeditions to the Himalayas, the Andes and other great mountain ranges of the world.

Being so fond of the open air, Germans are also enthusiastic campers—week-end campers as well as holiday campers. Not only do they take their tents and caravans to beauty spots in their own country, but thousands of West Germans go off south in search of the summer sun and the·beaches; over the Brenner Pass into Italy, to Spain and to other Mediterranean countries. As campers they are very well organised and equipped.

Hiking and youth-hostelling are favourite outdoor activities. Here, a group of young hikers are taking a well-earned rest on the steps of this ancient building, now used as a youth hostel

There is a lot of water in and around Germany: the sea coasts of the Baltic and the North Sea, the rivers, the lakes of central and southern Germany. All this water is used not only by shipping or for the production of electricity but also by ordinary people for recreation. By the sea and on the lakes many enthusiasts go in for yachting in anything from large cruisers which take part in ocean-racing to small dinghies which families bring to the water on top of their cars. Quite a few world championships in various dinghy classes have been held on Lake Constance and the large Bavarian lakes. On the rivers canoeing and rowing are also popular.

Many other types of sport are enjoyed by people in Germany: swimming, angling, ball games, shooting, hunting (deer and wild boar), athletics, gliding and gymnastics; and, in winter, skiing, tobogganing and skating. On winter weekends roads teem with cars carrying skis strapped to their roofs, making their way to the Black Forest, the Harz Mountains or the Bavarian Alps for a few days' skiing. German Railways even run special wintersports excursion trains.

Active sports play a very important part in the lives of Germany's young people. Germans are almost as keen on sport and exercise as the Ancient Greeks were. They believe that a healthy mind can only exist in a healthy body, and that physical exercise is one certain way of remaining healthy and happy.

Physical education is a compulsory subject in German schools right up to the end of secondary school. In East Germany the government takes a hand in urging all people, young and old alike, to take up an active sport. About two-thirds of the whole population of East Germany practises some sport or other. This is a very high percentage by comparison with other countries. In West Germany, too, every town and village has its sports clubs and public facilities such as running-tracks, football grounds, indoor and outdoor swimming-pools. Many clubs even run physical training classes for toddlers.

As you might expect, Germany has a highly successful record in the Olympic Games. In recent years the combined German team from East and West Germany has won numerous gold, silver and bronze medals in many sports, among them sailing, horse-riding, football, figure-skating, athletics and ski-jumping. Since 1968, East and West Germany have each sent separate teams to the Olympic Games.

Of course, many people do not like being energetic, at least not all the time. They would rather watch a sport—be

A thoughtful group before the start of a cycle race. Perhaps they are wondering what their chances are

In Germany, even very young children perform in track events. These professional-looking runners are all under ten years of age

spectators. The most popular spectator sport in Germany is football. Matches are played on both Saturdays and Sundays. As in many other countries, the crowds get wildly enthusiastic. For national championships and international matches they turn out in their thousands, singing, cheering and waving. It is fortunate that there are some very large stadia in Germany in which the most important matches can be played. Those in Berlin, Frankfurt and Stuttgart each seat over 90,000 people.

Other popular spectator sports which attract vast numbers of supporters are motor-car and motor-cycle racing. The Solitude (near Stuttgart) and Nürburgring (in the Eifel Mountains) tracks are only two of many race-tracks which are internationally famous. Equally well-known are the makes of German racing machines: *Mercedes* and *Porsche* for cars, *NSU* and *BMW* for motor-cycles.

There are many other ways, too, in which German people like to spend their leisure time. They go to the theatre or cinema; they sing in choirs, go dancing, listen to records; and very often they sit in cafés over cups of steaming coffee and huge slices of rich cream cake, just talking. Most Germans love to talk and argue simply for the fun of it. The men argue about politics, work and football results, and the women gossip about neighbours, clothes and children, just as people do everywhere else in the world. It is quite normal to ask one's friends round for a glass of wine and a chat in the evening. In the winter the local inn, like the English pub, attracts a good crowd every evening; many men go there to play bowls or cards. But most Germans like their homes, and many of them

Not all leisure activities take place out-of-doors. Chess is very popular in Germany and is treated seriously—as can be seen from these young East Berlin competitors

prefer to stay in during the evening. Television certainly has a lot to do with families wanting to stay at home at night. So does reading; there are always plenty of books and magazines in German homes, for they are great readers in their spare time.

Most Germans like to be gay and enjoy one another's company. Fortunately, there are many opportunities for them to do so. Every region, practically every town and village, has its traditional fairs, festivals and processions, for which people turn out in large numbers to celebrate a seasonal or historical event, or simply to eat, drink and be merry. Most country districts celebrate the bringing-in of the harvest with a great get-together at which huge slabs of cake and gallons of beer and wine are served on tables in the open air or under a marquee, and dancing goes on until late at night. Some of the major fairs last a week or longer. Munich (in Bavaria), famous for its breweries, has its annual *Oktoberfest*, a beer festival in October which lasts for two weeks and which is attended by visitors from far and wide. It is held in a vast fairground and offers everything from shooting stalls, switch-backs, merry-go-rounds and halls of mirrors to enormous beer tents in which people sit at long tables drinking beer out of pottery mugs and singing to the accompaniment of brass bands. The Bavarians, of course, are very hearty people who can consume large quantities of beer and Munich sausages. Stuttgart has a similar traditional fun-fair, which grew up from what was originally just an agricultural fair to which farmers brought their cattle and horses, and manufacturers their tractors and other farm machinery in order to sell them.

Further north, on the Rhine, the Main and in the Palatinate, there are the autumn wine festivals. They are to celebrate the bringing-in of the grape harvest and to taste the new wine. They are very gay events, with much dancing and drinking. Some last for several days, like the big German Wine Festival in October at which the German Wine Queen is elected.

At carnival time everyone dresses up and people often dance through the streets all night

Later in the year the carnival season begins. This is celebrated in most parts of Germany but especially on the Rhine and in Munich. The origin of this carnival is a religious one. On the Tuesday before Lent it used to be customary to indulge in much eating, drinking and merry-making in preparation for the fast which had to be observed during Lent. Gradually the day lost its religious significance, and the feasting spread over a much longer period; now carnival officially starts on 11th November at 11.11 p.m. Between then and Ash Wednesday it is customary for all sorts of clubs, associations and private individuals to organise fancy-dress balls. It is just an excuse to while away the dreary winter months. The highlights of carnival are the celebrated fancy-dress balls and street processions in Cologne and Mainz on the Monday and Tuesday before Lent. Even Germans living abroad come back to Germany specially for these events.

Life in Modern Germany

Among the most noticeable distinctions between East and West Germany are the differences in the way people live. Despite great efforts, East Germany has not succeeded in catching up with West Germany's standard of living. Not as many people own cars; many have more modest homes; they do not have expensive holidays abroad; and the East German shops are not filled with the same glittering displays of goods that can be seen in West Germany.

Since private ownership of property is discouraged in Communist East Germany, there are no really rich people such as large land- or property-owners. The families with the highest incomes are usually those in which both mother and father work in skilled jobs.

Flats in the centre of East Berlin, showing distinct Russian influence in their design. Note the difference between these flats and those in Munich shown on the facing page

A modern housing development in Munich, in West Germany

In both parts of Germany ordinary people are well housed. However, rents are very much higher in the West than the East. But, of course, wages in West Germany are much higher on average.

An interesting fact is that in both parts of Germany, and especially in and around towns, most people live in flats— either in large blocks or in houses divided into two, three or more flats. The more modern of these flats have balconies which the flat-dwellers use for sunbathing, drying clothes and growing flowers in pots and boxes. Both town and country people in Germany are very fond of window-boxes filled with masses of brightly-coloured geraniums, petunias and begonias. Another way in which town people living in flats make up for their lack of a garden is by growing house-plants in pots. A

71

window filled entirely with house-plants is a very common sight in German flats and houses.

Since individual houses, occupied by one family only, are so expensive, there are far fewer of these than there are flats. In West Germany these so-called "one-family houses" are usually found only in the fashionable suburbs of large cities, where rich business people live, and in the attractive holiday areas where people buy weekend houses or houses to live in when they retire.

Double-glazed windows are to be found in most German flats and houses; they are necessary because the winters are often quite severe, especially in the mountain regions. Incidentally, it is not usual for German families to have their windows cleaned on the outside by a window-cleaner. They find it very easy to clean their own windows because the windows open inwards and can therefore be cleaned from the inside. Many of the modern flats are designed with attractive features such as large picture-windows, central heating, lifts, rubbish shoots, laundries in the basements and gardens on the roofs. Sometimes there is also a caretaker to look after the heating and cleaning.

West Germany is amongst the countries of the world which have the highest number of motor-cars per head of the population. It is a country where life almost seems to be ordered by the motor-car. Town streets are tremendously busy and noisy; and people stream out to the countryside at weekends; at holiday-time, too, many people go by car.

East Germany, by comparison, has far fewer cars at present, but numbers are rising very fast.

The majority of West Germans get at least three weeks' holiday each year, and many people now get four weeks. There are also a number of public holidays throughout the year which come as a welcome interruption to work, such as Ascension Day (thirty-nine days after Easter), May Day (1st May), Unity Day (17th June) and, of course, the religious holidays in the autumn and at Christmas. Thousands of West Germans spend their holidays in Spain and other Mediterranean countries.

East Germans get shorter holidays. As they are not allowed to travel to the West, those who do go abroad go to Czechoslovakia or one of the other East European countries. A popular holiday for East German workers is a fortnight in one of the many trade union holiday centres.

Most shops in East Germany belong either to the government-administered H.O. *(Handelsorganisation)* or to the Co-operative movement. There are many self-service shops and quite a few large stores in the major cities. But none of them is as well stocked with goods as the shops in the West. A favourite leisure occupation of West Germans is to stroll through the modern shopping centres, window-shopping and gazing at all the wonderful displays of goods. Food shops are among the most fascinating throughout both East and West Germany: the butchers' shops with their carefully cut and tastefully displayed pieces of meat and their dozens of different kinds

73

Sausages of all shapes and sizes greet the eye of the shopper in most German butchers' shops

of sausages in all shapes and sizes; the general stores with their bewildering arrays of wines and preserves, fruit and sweets; the bakers and confectioners with their many different types of white, brown and black bread, their gorgeous fruit and cream cakes and their local specialities such as salt *Pretzeln* in southern Germany or sultana tea-bread in Westphalia.

Food is certainly taken seriously in Germany. People like

eating well, and women who do not go to work spend quite a large part of their day in the kitchen preparing home-made dishes for their families, baking cakes for the weekend and making jam in summer. Of course, tinned and frozen food is becoming more and more popular with the many women who go to work and have to cook a meal very quickly when they get home at night. At lunch-time people who go to work either take sandwiches from home or eat in the works canteen. Most large- and medium-sized firms run a canteen where their staff can sit down to a well-cooked meal.

The belief that Germans eat nothing but *Sauerkraut* (pickled cabbage), sausages and potato soup is as widespread as it is false. German cooking may not be as artistic nor as celebrated as French cooking, but on the other hand it is not as plain as, for example, English cooking. And it is certainly varied. Every region has its own specialities: onion tart in Swabia, pigs' trotters in Berlin, fish dishes on the coast. But restaurants also serve what is called "international cuisine", such as roast chicken, steak and *pommes frites* (chips). The meat sold by butchers in Germany is very good but rather expensive; this is why many German housewives do not serve meat every day. Instead, they cook dishes made from vegetables, eggs or cheese. Fried potatoes with salad, or noodles with tomato sauce would be considered quite a satisfactory evening meal by many families.

Eating out, especially at weekends, is a well-loved custom. This is partly the reason why German restaurant cooking, on the whole, is good, often as good as home cooking. In summer people like to drive into the countryside and have a Sunday meal at a country inn, or at least coffee and cakes in an open-air café.

They like to dress up and look smart on Sundays, even if they are going nowhere in particular. This is just one of the traditional formalities. Another is the general politeness of people towards each other. Some customs, like men raising their hats when greeting another person or children curtseying to adults, are fast dying out. But it is still customary to greet friends and acquaintances with a handshake and Germans always pass the time of day when meeting someone. It would be considered very bad manners not to do so. Even in shops

Vegetable dishes are popular in Germany. Here, German housewives wait to be served at an open-air market stall

(not large shops or self-service stores, of course) it is usual to say the ceremonious *Guten Tag* (Good-day) and *Auf Wiedersehen* (Good-bye).

Christian names are only used among close relatives and very good friends. It takes a long time before older people stop calling each other Mr. X or Mrs. Y, and then the ceremony of exchanging Christian names is usually conducted over a glass of wine. The German language, like French, has two different words for "you". *Du* is used for close friends and members of the family, *Sie* for strangers or people who are merely acquaintances.

Religion plays an important part in the lives of many people in Germany, both young and old. There are two main denominations: Protestant and Roman Catholic. In the West there are slightly more Protestants than Catholics, in the East there are seven times as many Protestants as Catholics. It can therefore be said that Germany is a predominantly Protestant country. Most of West Germany's Catholics live in the south of the country; Bavaria, for example, is almost entirely Catholic.

Everybody in Germany is allowed freedom of choice in religious matters, though in East Germany the policy of the communist government is to encourage atheism in the hope that, as time goes by, fewer and fewer people will go to church.

Art and Science

What Europe enjoys today in the way of scientific achievements, of literature, music and art, in short what we call European civilisation has been contributed to by many nations. Germany's part in it is a very important one. She produced many of the great men who have become famous throughout the world for inventing and discovering things, for writing books and music and creating works of art.

Germany has often been called "a land of poets and thinkers", but her chief fame probably lies in the field of music. There cannot be many people in the western world who do not know the names of some German composers and have not heard their music, although they may never really have given a thought to the composers' nationality. The three great *B*s, for example, are easily remembered: Bach, Beethoven and Brahms.

There were many others, too, who count among the world's great composers. They include George Frederick Handel (who

Music plays a very important role in the cultural life of Germany and many people enjoy going to concerts. This is the scene in the Berlin State Opera House during a performance

was a German from Halle, although he lived in England for much of his life), Felix Mendelssohn, and Robert Schumann; the two opera composers—Richard Wagner and Richard Strauss; and, in more recent times, such composers as Paul Hindemith and Carl Orff.

Some of the German orchestras playing the works of these

and other composers have become equally famous—for example, the Berlin Philharmonic Orchestra and the Leipzig Gewandhaus Orchestra. And their conductors too are world-famous.

Let us turn for a brief moment to the "poets and thinkers", among whom we should, of course, include novelists, playwrights and philosophers. Many of them have become widely known beyond the borders of their home country, more particularly the philosophers Immanuel Kant, Friedrich Nietzsche and Arthur Schopenhauer (during the eighteenth and nineteenth centuries), and the political philosopher Karl Marx, whose writings have been translated into far more languages than the Bible. Two great poets and playwrights whose popularity almost matches that of Shakespeare are Johann Wolfgang von Goethe (1749–1832) and Friedrich von Schiller (1759–1805). In more recent times, there are the playwrights Gerhard Hauptmann (who won a Nobel Prize in 1912) and Berthold Brecht whose *Threepenny Opera* is one of the world's most famous pieces for the stage; and the novelist Thomas Mann, who won a Nobel Prize in 1924. His books have been translated into many languages.

Among the greatest artists of Germany's past is Albrecht Dürer (1471–1528). He produced the most marvellous woodcuts as well as drawings and copper engravings. Hans Holbein the Younger, who painted, among other things, a very famous portrait of Henry VIII of England, was one of the masters of sixteenth-century painting. The fifteenth and sixteenth centuries seem to have been particularly rich in German artists. In more recent times, too, Germans have again played leading roles in the field of art.

The most important German figure in this century in the field of art is probably Walter Gropius, who has now become one of America's greatest architects. He was responsible for building the Bauhaus, an art school, at Dessau in 1925. This has been described as the first truly modern piece of architecture. More than this, though, the Bauhaus (directed by Gropius) revolutionised modern art with its teaching principles.

The part played by ordinary people in the cultural life of the country must also be mentioned. Many of them go regularly to the theatre—more than in most other European countries. There are fine theatres in all the large towns, as well as a lot of folk theatres in the country, where operas and plays are performed throughout the year. Needless to say, they always play to full houses.

A very large number of people learn to play musical instruments. Many of them learn how to play as children at school. Consequently there are plenty of local amateur orchestras, whose performances are as good as those of professionals. The Germans, too, love singing just as much as the Welsh do and there are choirs in all the towns and villages, often connected with the churches. Music festivals are held in a large number of centres every year. Some of them achieve world-wide recognition. Naturally, with such great musical interest the Germans are keen concert-goers and all their orchestras are well supported.

Most German towns of any size have their own art galleries. These display not only the works of national artists, but also a wide selection of art from all over the world.

The German sense of design is well expressed in many German homes. Decorations and furnishings are chosen carefully so that they do not clash. Throughout the country, culture clearly has a very marked effect on public taste.

A doctor's family enjoying a musical evening together. Each member of the family plays a different instrument

Lunch-hour practice. Most villages, towns and even factories have their own bands

It is not surprising that an almost landlocked country (one with only very short coastlines) should have played only a small part in the exploration of the world. Throughout the centuries, the majority of Germans have preferred to stay at home or, at least, in Europe. Their energies have been directed towards scientific discoveries rather than geographical ones and to inventing useful things.

Among the many things with which German scientists and inventors have been connected two things are outstanding. Firstly, there is the part they played in the development of the motor-car. Although they did not invent it alone, they had a tremendous influence on its early development. Secondly, there is the field of atomic research. Germans played their part in the discovery of nuclear fission.

The story of the motor-car begins with the work of Dr. Nikolaus Otto of Cologne. He designed an engine driven by a mixture of gas and air and this, in turn, formed the basis of the petrol engine invented by Gottlieb Daimler. Daimler built one of the first successful cars in the 1880s. During the same period another successful car was developed by Karl Benz of Mannheim. The two men eventually joined forces to form the now-famous Daimler-Benz company, which has been one of the world's leading car manufacturers ever since. The company still has its headquarters in Stuttgart.

Another German, Rudolf Diesel, was the inventor of the Diesel engine which was developed during the early years of this century. At that time, too, German names were becoming world-famous in the field of flight—notably Count Ferdinand von Zeppelin (airships built on his design, called Zeppelins, were used during the First World War), and Hugo Junkers. In the field of science the most well-known German names are those of Otto Hahn (the man who worked with uranium) and Wernher von Braun, the inventor of the rockets which put America's astronauts into space. These two scientists both grew up in Germany and later lived and worked in the United States.

As far back as the fifteenth century Germans were producing

inventions which were to change the lives of people throughout the world. In 1444, at Mainz, Johann Gutenberg set up the first printing press with movable type. Thus he made the cheaper printing of books possible and is recognised as the inventor of printing.

Then there was the brilliant astronomer Johannes Kepler who lived between 1571 and 1630. He discovered how the planets move and set down his theories in three rules known as Kepler's Laws. Some say he also invented the astronomical telescope.

In the following century there was the equally well-known German scientist Gabriel Fahrenheit (though to tell the truth he lived for most of his life in England and Holland). He gave his name to the Fahrenheit thermometer which has a temperature scale with freezing-point at 32 degrees and boiling-point at 212 degrees.

In the nineteenth century when the Industrial Revolution came to Germany there were, of course, many great names in science.

Werner von Siemens (1816–1892) was one of the leading pioneers in the use of electricity in industry. One of his greatest achievements was in connection with the telegraph system and he was responsible for laying the first great underground cables from Berlin to Frankfurt-am-Main. In 1866 he invented the dynamo. His brother William, who settled in England, is equally famous. His firm laid the transatlantic telegraph cable in 1874 and he was a well-known inventor. Today, the

name of Siemens is still important in the electrical industry—
it is the name of one of the leading manufacturers of electric
cables and machinery.

Then there was Robert Bunsen, a chemist who discovered
several new elements and invented the Bunsen burner, now
used in all chemical laboratories. This burner is also the basis
of all our modern gas-cookers and gas-fires. Another famous
chemist was Justus von Liebig who introduced artificial
fertilisers. Any farmer will tell you just how important they
are today.

A man whose name you will find on any good map of the
Pacific Ocean was Alexander von Humboldt. The Humboldt
Current flows off the coast of Equador and Peru. Working at
the end of the eighteenth century and well into the nineteenth
he was a natural scientist of world-wide reputation. He
travelled everywhere and was interested in geology, oceano-
graphy and botany, as well as making a special study of the
magnetism of the earth. Today the university in East Berlin
is named after him.

The nineteenth century also brought great discoveries in
medicine. The causes of the diseases cholera and tuberculosis
were unknown until Robert Koch (1843–1910) came on the
scene. For his work he was awarded a Nobel Prize in 1905.
Another doctor, Emil von Behring, was awarded a Nobel
Prize in 1901 for discovering serums to combat diphtheria
and tetanus (blood poisoning). But the discovery which has
had perhaps the widest use in medicine came in 1895 when

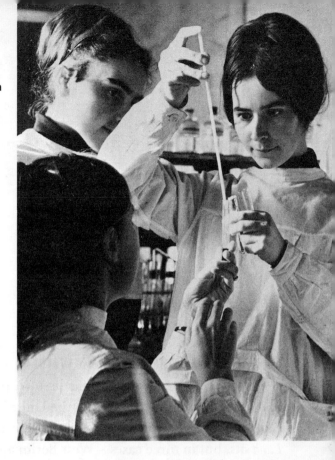

Wilhelm Röntgen (Nobel Prize-winner in 1901) found the
properties of X-rays. These are still called Röntgen rays in
Germany.

German scientists and inventors continue to be very much
in the forefront of the world's progress.

How Germany is Governed

For the purposes of government West Germany is divided into eleven *Länder* each of which has its own parliament. A *Land* may be compared with a state in the United States of America. Each *Land* has a capital city where the parliament of that *Land* sits, but in three cases—West Berlin and the ancient Free Cities of Bremen and Hamburg—the *Land* is little bigger than the city itself. The largest *Land* in area is Bavaria with its capital at Munich; the smallest is the Saarland with its capital at Saarbrücken.

The *Länder* are divided into *Landkreise*, or counties, and they in turn are divided into *Gemeinden*, or communes. They are supervised by the *Länder* governments, but they look after their own local affairs such as building, schools, cultural matters and social welfare.

Although the *Länder* have a large degree of self-government and are wholly responsible for education, the police force and the maintenance of law and order, there still has to be a central government to look after things which affect the country as a whole. These are matters such as foreign policy, defence, postal services, railways, currency, taxation and the making of the laws. The important thing to remember, though, is that nothing can be done without the consent of the *Länder*.

The central parliament is made up of two houses: the *Bundestag* and the *Bundesrat*. The *Bundestag* is the body which makes the laws and governs the country as a whole. It consists of 518 members. The head of the *Bundestag* is called the Chancellor of the Federal Republic. He is elected by the party (or group of parties working together—known as a coalition) which has the majority of members in the *Bundestag*. At the time of writing Dr. Kurt Georg Kiesinger is Chancellor. The best-known and most influential Federal Chancellor since the Second World War has been Dr. Konrad Adenauer.

Elections for the *Bundestag* take place every four years. Voters must be at least 18 years old and candidates 21 years years old.

The second house of parliament is called the *Bundesrat*. This consists of forty-five members appointed by the *Länder* governments. The duty of the *Bundesrat* is to represent the *Länder* in the central government and make sure that there is co-operation between the *Länder* governments and the *Bundestag*.

The **Bundeshaus** (parliament building) of the West German Government

The head of state in West Germany is called the Federal President and he is elected for a five-year term. At the time of writing he is Dr. Heinrich Lübke.

EAST GERMANY

In East Germany there is no political point of view represented in the parliament other than that of the socialists; since 1952 the country has been governed by what is called a National Front. The National Front consists of five political parties, all of them left-wing socialist, communist in fact, plus the trade unions, youth movements, women's league and the cultural league. Instead of representing different political points of view, the parties represent different groups of people in the community, such as workers, farmers and so on.

The highest body in the government is the People's Chamber; the members of this chamber are elected every four years. Voters must be 18 years old at least and candidates 21 years old. None of the members is a professional politician. They are all part-time and voluntary members. There are 434 seats which are shared among the parties in proportion to the amount of support they are thought to have in the country.

Most of the major decisions in government are made by the State Council, which is a committee of twenty-four members, elected by the People's Chamber every four years. The Chairman of the State Council is, in effect, the head of state, since the position of President was abolished a short time ago. At the time of writing, the Chairman of the State Council is Walter Ulbricht.

In addition, there is a Council of Ministers which is responsible for seeing that the economic and social decisions of the People's Chamber and the State Council are put into operation. The Council of Ministers organises and controls the whole planning of the economic system and is the most important body in home affairs.

The central government as described above has absolute control and can reverse or alter any decisions made by local councils in the regions or towns. In fact, any higher authority can change the decisions of any authority lower down the scale.

The country is divided into fifteen regions, each of which is administered by a regional council. The regions are further sub-divided into counties or large towns which themselves have councils which are responsible to the regional council. At the bottom of the "pyramid" there are the villages and small towns whose councils are responsible to those of the counties and large towns.

Index